THE SOUL OF WIT

Also by Ralph McInerny from St. Augustine's Press and Dumb Ox Books

POETRY

Shakespearean Variations

PROSE

The Defamation of Pius XII
Let's Read Latin: Introduction to the Language of the Church

TRANSLATIONS

John of St. Thomas, *Introduction to the Summa Theologiae of Thomas Aquinas*
Thomas Aquinas, *Disputed Questions on Virtue*
Florent Gaboriau, *The Conversion of Edith Stein*

INTRODUCTIONS, PREFACES, OR FOREWORDS

Fulvio di Blasi, *God and the Natural Law: A Rereading of Thomas Aquinas*
George A. Kelly, *The Second Spring of the Church in America*
Josef Pieper, *Happiness and Contemplation*
Robert Hugh Benson, *Lord of the World*
Thomas Aquinas, *Commentary on Aristotle's De Anima*
Thomas Aquinas, *Commentary on Aristotle's Nicomachean Ethics*
Thomas Aquinas, *Commentary on Aristotle's Metaphysics*
Thomas Aquinas, *Commentary on Aristotle's Physics*
Thomas Aquinas, *Commentary on Aristotle's On Interpretation*
Timothy L. Smith, ed., *Faith and Reason*
Michael M. Waddell, ed., *Restoring Nature: Essays in Thomistic Philosophy and Theology*
Timothy L. Smith, ed., *Aquinas's Sources: The Notre Dame Symposium*
John O'Callaghan, ed., *Science, Philosophy, and Theology*

The Soul of Wit

Ralph McInerny

ST. AUGUSTINE'S PRESS
South Bend, Indiana
2005

1 2 3 4 5 6   10 09 08 07 06 05

Library of Congress Cataloging in Publication Data
McInerny, Ralph M.
    The soul of wit / Ralph McInerny.
        p. cm.
    ISBN 1-58731-803-2 (pbk. : alk. paper)
    I. Title.
    PS3563.A31166S67 2004
    811'.54 – dc22   2004017637

∞ *The paper used in this publication meets the minimum requirements of
the American National Standard for Information Sciences – Permanence
of Paper for Printed Materials, ANSI Z39.48-1984.*

ST. AUGUSTINE'S PRESS
www.staugustine.net

Contents

I

A DONNE DEAL

The finger that the ring is on
a circling golden band
pads with flesh the nether bone
and hides the skeleton of the hand.

Bone remains when flesh is gone
shuffled into dust
and so the ring remains upon
the finger, as is just.

MOTES

Seen from another room
a door ajar admits
an angled bar of sun
in which the dusty spirits
dance and sparkle bright.
The particles in random flight,
a cosmos for the nonce,
suggest that only chance
controls their antics. Now sun
eclipsed by cloud is gone
but dust invisible still sits
in air. The momentary flurry
spelled memento mori.

FOR THE BIRDS

Young trees grow in wood chipped islands
in a parking lot, their bottoms wrapped
like babies, wanting water, as curl
of leaf and droop of branch attest.
You would not bet a nickel on their future
flourishing, but I predict the day will come
when birds descend in parabolic swoops
to muster in their branches and protest
that Kilmer was here, shamelessly robbing nests.

EASY ESSE

To be a bee presents no task
for them, busy buzzing back
and forth, pollinating flowers,
making honey at all hours.

Midwives in my garden linger
a menace with their stinger,
their ultimate end remains unseen,
a hived and hidden queen.

ABROAD

Italy encouraged Browning's British eye
To see a monk who failed to keep his vows
And sought the joys that flesh bestows,
A well-hung duke whose duchess had an eye
Too soon made glad, a bishop without faith,
Fine foreign instances of fallen man.
I wonder why his home thoughts never ran
To clerics such as Trollope's whose only faith
Was that of gentlemen, whose reach did not exceed
Their grasp, since grasping was their creed.

EASTER THOUGHTS

You can't take it with you
the gold and the glitter
or eggs that beneath you
nestle in promise of later.

Houses and cars you will leave
baubles of whatever kind
nor does money interest the grave
the safest investment is land.

The plot that receives you is yours
though body decay into dust
the marker that says so will last
while planets still move in their course.

Elsewhere your soul will await
to claim the dust that lies here
some day that is distant or near
you shall rise to your real estate.

ADDENDA

The gallows in my garden
glows with flowers
they hanging pray for pardon
an extension of their hours.

If I were God and could relent
and halt their death
both they and I'd repent
and curse the caught breath

that stopped the petal's fall.
The apparent good
of permanence, to bud
allowed, would every bloom forestall.

The rose that cannot wither
is rose no more,
life is the before
of easeful death, as mother

the child was of another
mother, and on
and on and on:
as well ask for changeless weather.

——I

So let the roses die
I acquiesce,
I do, and bless
their serial eternity.

IN VIA

Along a cemetery road made
indistinct by fallen leaves
a chubby jogger huffs and puffs
defying death among the dead.

Each breath might be her last,
escape among the monuments
and join the enormous silence
that gathers over listening dust.

For now, her heart pumps on,
her sneakers hit the road
whose end she would postpone.
As we would if we could.

VALUES

Pictures on the wall of this motel
convey some nowhere in pastel;
guests unpack and spend the night
then go off down the interstate
to places surely far more real
than those here framed upon the wall.

I wonder who produces them.
One no doubt whose youthful dream
was of high art, perhaps of fame.
I hunt among the pastels for his name.
It is not there, as if in shame
he painted and would not claim
their authorship. *Nemo pinxit*,
and cursed be he who thinks it
art. Burnt umber, vermillion, ochre,
can color too the mediocre
but when ambition deserts the will
it's wise to settle for pastel.

Or does he mock unseeing eyes
blind to nature as well as art?
And who am I to criticize
with my lacey pastel heart?

SIC ET NON

Cada uno es artifice de sa ventura
So do not blame the gods or fate.
Each fashions his own fortune, sirrah,
There's no one else you can berate.

Of course the saying's false,
Our actions spring from impulse
Or other thoughtless cause
That frames our future with extrinsic laws.

Or maybe some of each,
Our life a book in which
We mean to write one story
And write another. And are sorry.

II

LAKE CITY

The dust from which I came lies buried
here, my family name engraved upon
this stone, and here lies too the maid he married,
both unknown to me the distant son

of sons of sons. My family tree is rooted
here in earth and I a withering branch
stand lost in muddled wonder, within an inch
of worms myself, thought and feeling muted.

Plots thicken on the earth and buried bones
support a later flesh till we and they
are called by Him who all our sins atones
to that dreaded, longed for judgment day.

WATER COLOR

The chair in which all those years ago
she sat sits still, and on the wall
behind, its image hangs, painted by
my father – the empty chair, a shawl across
its arm, a braided oval rug beneath.

If you would know the color of water, cry,
the past is better seen with moistened eye.

THESE ARE PEARLS THAT WERE HIS EYES

My father from the mirror looks back
at me and on my face my hand
can feel the shape of his. Just so
my son in future silvered glass
will peer at me and wonder where
his self begins and when if ever
he and he alone exists.

Reflected to infinity
God's image gazes back at Him.

PRESERVES

The kitchen full of steam and on the stove
kettles of tomatoes boiling. Late summer
in Minneapolis, my mother canning
against the winter, a houseful of kids,
money short, my dad wherever the work was.
Mason jars, their lead tops sealed
with rubber rings, fill the shelves, abundance,
and a weary aproned woman sits down at last
to rest.
      May she still rest in peace
all these years later, though years don't count
where she is now, all her canned goods
entered to her account in the Book of Life.

TYRO

I practiced on a paper keyboard
flat upon the table
it was all we could afford
and I was far from able

and yet I thought it would be grand
an audible instrument to play
my imagined talent on display
upright in pianoland.

Marvelous music never heard,
one of a host of hopes
most of them absurd
while I slid down life's slopes.

NECKING

At sixteen in my father's post-war Chevrolet
I drove to Pilot's Knob to park
and hug and kiss a pliant girl
up to no good in the dark.

It is our innocence that stays,
prelapsarian almost,
lips on lips and little else.
Someone married a girl who'd only been kissed.

My timid hand on her soft sweater
felt beneath her softer breast
and that was all. Was it ignorance
or innocence? No matter, I'm impressed.

GRANDMA RUSH

Become a guest in her own home
coddled by a child she bore
she sipped her tea as I sat dumb
listening to what had been before.

Birch Cooley, Morton, memories,
her soft voice told the beads
of past. I listened to her stories,
I hear them still, the doers and the deeds

that somehow in my blood
continue, though she's dead.

IN OUR BEGINNING

The Plains of Abraham were thick with snow
on that Epiphany when we just wed
arrived where Michael was conceived
and born and christened that same year.
In Sillery first, then on the Avenue des Braves,
we clung together till, again in winter,
you went off to *Hôpital Saint Sacrement*
and in a full day's pain brought forth
our son. 'O Mine Papa" was crooned
by Eddie Fisher, the bells of *Saintes Martyres*
rang out, and at the *Aux Delices* with George Lavere
I toasted with Canadian beer
our entry into parenthood,
the joy that would be bracketed with pain.

REXFORD DRIVE

Belafonte sang calypso while
we rolled beige paint upon the walls of our
first home in April 1957
just two months after Michael died.
We felt his absence in that house he never saw
I held you and we wept for our dead son.
He lies reburied now in Cedar Grove
on the campus where we lived
and we will lie there with him bye and bye.

III

NAZARETH HALL

At school from a pulpit niched
into the wall the Martyrology was read
to boys awaiting lunch, and while they ate
the images of racks and wheels and fire
prepared them for the long digestion
of truths for which they hoped to die.
Waiters brought on trays the heads
of witnesses, among the tables mortal
boys moved toward their later lunch.
All that was a half a century since.
How many now lie dead of natural causes,
disease, jammed hearts, or accident,
of anything but Dioclitean cruelty?

LEAVING HOME

My mother made my bed before she left
and other mothers in the freshman dorm fussed over
sons, loath to leave though finally they did.
Later, in the long lightless room, in bed,
we felt their fussing come back from everywhere they'd gone
bringing home that we were on our own.

The wind from off the lake cried at the windows
and in the rows of beds set head to head
cheeks on the cheeks of pillows sought the softness
of a mother's and I mimicked the wind.
A dozen years it took to reach the age
when I would lie alone in a strange place
out of the womb for good alas forever.

FESTINA LENTE

The rows of desks in study hall
had lids that lifted to display
the calenders on which each day
we made an X to hurry fall

along, then spring, as if release
from present time meant bliss,
Thanksgiving, Christmas, the endless peace
of summer happiness.

How odd in retrospect impatience
with the present seems
when I so want renascence
of all my youthful dreams.

ET IN ARCADIA EGO

Boys construed the Aeneid
in a basement classroom
whose sills were flush
with earth and windows gave upon
a courtyard where the sun
played over a garden lush
with flowers, ripening to their doom,
answering to the youth we had.

Virgil addressed a reader
like Augustus, responsive to his lines,
savoring the voyage that from Troy
brought his hero on to Rome. Dido
we halfway understood – lied to,
left, a holocaust, *vestigia flammae*,
while Aeneas ignored the smoky signs
of his betrayal nor felt a traitor.

Little Latin and less Greek had we
but phrases some intimation gave
of all that lay in wait, an Italy
of the heart in which the tears of things
would weep in us. Sadness brings
again that happy past not yet fully
understood, when parsing boys, brave
with ignorance, embarked on a wine-dark sea.

ANGELUS

The rough rope when pulled
tipped the bell that pealed
and pulsed throughout the school

while we upon our knees would pray
the Angelus each day
at noon, our Aves jewel

strung on the string of time
recurrent as a rhyme
echoing soft avowals.

On the baldachino words
in Latin, only lately surds,
now announced Annunciation

and boys alert to an inner voice
were like the Maid whose fiat's choice
both then and now spells our salvation.

MAY PROCESSION

The road before the school went down
a graveled way to where a bridge
joined an island on whose ridge
a chapel held the corpse of some

forgotten benefactor. In May,
in Mary's month, we boys went there
in straggling lines to say
our mindless prattling prayer.

The year like us was in its spring
and death was but a word,
life and we and birds must sing,
perhaps our prayers were heard.

The lazy water lapped the shore
and doubtless does today
but all that was and is no more
is but remembered May.

DECIDUOUS DAYS

Sap recedes and leaves
disengaging fall
on lawn, on shrubs, in eaves,
and far off freight trains call.

Days grow short in winter
the angle of the sun
is now somewhat off center,
cold sands slowly run.

Distant clatter on a bridge
arrives on frozen air,
and parallels converge
to meet in some nowhere.

NOVIAS Y NOVICIOS

Aspiring eunuchs we
mere apprentice celibates
untouched as yet by puberty
and its attendant loves or hates.

Can the innocent forego
pleasures they can only know
by loss of innocence, say no
or yes or seedless sow?

As brides and grooms assent
to futures all unknown
novices consent
to what they've never known.

IV

BALLAD
September 25, 2001

She does not dye her silver hair
But wears it as a crown
And when she gardens in the yard
Or roars across the lawn
Going blade to blade with grass
Her flesh is golden brown.

No one would guess this lady bears
A burden few could carry
Or that there weigh upon her heart
Conceptions far from merry
Her mien suggests insouciance
Her countenance is unwary

But you and I can read within
And we can see her soul
And there we find the secret hid
Though buried deep as coal
The thought that nothing she can do
But time will take its toll.

On the wide horizon of her mind
There looms a menace grim

A fateful date approaches near
When she must sink or swim
A day that brings a cup to her
That's winking to the brim,

A metaphor of sorts that she
Despite what she appears
Has watched the seasons roll away
And heard the hollow cheers
And now must recognize she's known
Ten and three score years.

The young may mock her tragedy
The wise may wisely smile
Her husband who is scarcely wise
But past that stony mile
Quotes Cicero on growing old
And is as usual vile.

Sometimes she sits upon her deck
And watches golfers play
She hears their cries of glee or woe
Their folly on display
And then despite her better self
In whispers she will say:

'What matters brevity of life
Or length if that should be?"
In short, she finds herself soon sunk
In a morass that she
Had sworn forever to eschew
I mean philosophy.

But as they must to men and women
Large questions will arrive
Though she has fought the tendency
To ask why she's alive
And joked that she'll let what's to be
Bug hornets in their hive.

Throughout her life unwillingly
She's heard such questions put
She's listened to the endless fights
And what is more to boot
Has always known her grandma knew
What these poor fools sought.

She bore her children one by one
Beginning in Quebec
Till like a Roman matron she
With children did bedeck
Herself and whatshisname her mate
Yet was no nervous wreck.

The worm was in the apple though
And she could not ignore
That she no longer rose in wrath
And very seldom swore
At rabbits in her garden since she's lived
Ten years three score.

There may be those who chuckle when
Their birthday is recalled
And there are even merry wives
Denying they're appalled

—IV

To find the man they're married to
Is very nearly bald.

When I was young and she was younger
When we were in our prime
The measure of our age did not
Make living seem a crime
But now the shadows lengthen
And shorten up our time.

The thing about a ballad is
It can go on and on
But with a subject such as mine
Its conclusion is forgone
And I will end by saying that
I will always love you, Con.

V

MICROCOSM

The dying star is not required
to witness its descent to darkness,
years in mindless millions measured
it and only angels marked its

first burst *ex nihilo,*
or whatever antecedents God
chose to fabricate the halo
of its light that darkness could not hide.

The flower from seed to bloom
emerges mindlessly as well,
forget-me-nots do not recall
us or the walls on which they climb.

Golden lads and lassies must
Like chimney sweepers come to dust
but unlike fading stars or flowers
they both endure and count the hours.

LAST RITES

Charles Baudelaire inhaled the scents of *fleurs de mal*
        ignoring, it seems, divine decrees
and yet he lay beneath his funeral pall
        muni des sacrements d'église.

Belief must baffle minds that think
        assent should prove itself in deeds,
that logic of the lucid sort must link
        the minds and wills of thinking reeds.

Not so. God's mercy disobeys our laws
and we, thank God, are shriven without cause.

RETREAT

A Sabine farm with Lalage
Rome left far behind
chiaroscuro on the beige
hills that all around surround

the poet's redoubt as clouds and sun
compose their intricate odes;
no father is the patron,
only distance peace provides.

Horace, the twice freed slave's
son in precarious independence
by crafty obscurity saves
his soul from an emperor's indulgence.

A DIFFIDENT PROMETHEUS

Morning becomes electric
above a jagged light
precedes the thunder like a trick
and I am full of fright.

Modern man is said to feel
he's in control of things,
master of his woe and weal,
the puller of the strings.

Why, he could easily blow
the earth to kingdom come,
in petri dishes make his clone,
plan a trip to Mars, and go.

But lightning shakes this confidence
and thunder gives us pause
better light the frankincense
and praise a higher cause.

SAT EST VIXISSE

Do fruit flies think that it suffices
    to flit for hours only
enjoying momentary crises
    in seconds to be lonely?

Life lifts to noon before it sets
    fast or slow, what matter?
The evening brings the same regrets
    but please let them come later.

DISYLLABIC SONNET

The mind
contains
remains
beyond
the now
from which
its twitch
somehow
presents
the past
held fast
in tense:
future
nurture.

IF

If seasons lost their salt and clocks their spring
Then our unquartered year would know a dying fall
And days unclockwise would like cuckoos sing
If seasons lost their salt and clocks their spring.
Time across our face would never crawl
The noonday devil would be all in all
If seasons lost their salt and clocks their spring
Then our unquartered year would know a dying fall.

DIGITAL ANALOG

Count upon your fingers
Total up your toes
Cold will make them number
And rubicund your nose

Frozen digits calculate
And reckon winter's here
Against its flu innoculate
Needle up your fear.

But still the blood runs colder
And on the windows frost
Makes filigrees yet bolder
Which tell of summer lost.

NOON

No one, nor nun
nor priest, can gainsay
the devil who at midday
walks proud as the sun.

Hands join in prayer
as in the upper room
the twelve in base fear
cowered awaiting doom.

We look ante and post
meridiem until
the sun stops standing still
and we with it continue west.

OUR DAYS ARE LIKE SHADOWS

Call me Ishmael and I won't answer
So forget in the evening to call
Humans who end in death by cancer
Begin in a primal bawl.

So forget in the evening to call
Save the coin that calling costs,
Because of sun the shadows fall
Mottling men and beasts.

Humans end in death by cancer.
Is it morbid so to think?
The hidden sun negates man's fear
Laughter helps and so does drink.

Beginning in a primal bawl
We whine and dine our lives away
But oft in shadow the sober soul
Remembers to praise and pray.

SURVIVOR

His life has been a long goodbye
He's seen so many fade and die
Like Job whose servant brings
Him bad news only
He's now as lonely
As the bell a leper rings.

His life has been a long farewell
And if he seems to bear it well
Last apple on the limb
The question does arise
When eventually he dies
Who will say goodbye to him?

HIC IACET

Beneath the snow lie fallen leaves
dead grass below then graves.

Our lives begin as green as spring
the seasons turn and winter bring.

All life's layers lie upon
one another and this stone.

AT HER BEDSIDE

Ionescu's bald soprano earned
    a smile, as who should say
the bearded lady. Now radiation's burned
    away my darling's hair

to chase the carcinoma from her brain
    and chemicals to the rescue
come, dripping from bags to this refrain:
    I hate you, Ionescu.

PAGING DOCTOR JOHNSON

Her dying eyes admit the living world
and time's still measured on her pulse
but pedants claim her percepts all are false.
It is the sort of point on which she quarreled
a lot, the paradox of known
and knower. Is *esse* only *percipi*?
Nonsense, she'd say, what kind of noun
names only him who names? Xanthippe
she was not, but loved the tug of logos,
the flying shuttle with which we weave
our webs with no intention to deceive
or make canonical the bogus.
Her obsequies will be her Q.E.D.
The real earth receiving her she will not see.

RONDEAU

Gone is the glow from lip and cheek
     Our eyes are bright no more
The gifts we got we did not seek
     But feared a heart grown sore
And sinfully spent capital
     As we had done before.
Gone is the glow from lip and cheek
     Our eyes are bright no more.

EN RETARD

Dying young has its rewards.
Flaming flowers fade,
But he has lived too long for words
And shivers in the shade
Nor need he read entrails of birds
To guess where he'll be laid.

But he has lived too long for words
And shivers in the shade
The goats are separate now in herds
And debts must all be paid
Nor need he read entrails of birds
To guess where he'll be laid.

The goats are separate now in herds
And debts must all be paid
Angels of judgment draw their swords
As final accounts are made
Nor need he read entrails of birds
To guess where he'll be laid.

Angels of judgment draw their swords
As final accounts are made
And darker spirits in gathering hordes
Take those who disobeyed

Nor need he read entrails of birds
   To know where he'll be laid.

JUNIOR FUI ET SENUI

In the dead of night in a silent house
Alone in a crowded past
He sits. The chambers of his soul echo
With voices long since still, his children
Gone into a future already past,
His wife asleep in the night that awaits us all.
Hope like snow in spring has melted
His youth lies bottled in racks
Aging, collecting dust.
Oft remembered sorrows are sweet
As joys recalled are sad.
Il naufragar m'e dolce in questo mare.
He nods in his chair.
He was young and now he is old.

LEARNED IGNORANCE

Long ago I knew it all
or some significant percent
only ask and I would tell
the asker what was meant.

Things have changed and I am dumb
so Socrates move over
make room for one who now is mum
and runneth quick for cover.

Wisdom is the goal that we
pursue though willy-nilly
our reach exceeds our grasp and we
have ended merely silly.

MAKE ME CHASED, LORD

Lovers when they're lucky simply love
and are by their beloved loved in turn
they're not at all like figures on an urn
who chased and chasing cannot even move.
The poet when he casts his lines about
weighs words and chews upon his pen
imagining the lover's joy and pain
but cannot feel the awful ache of doubt.

An imaged love is measured out by feet,
by cadence, is even hung upon the wall
to stir at one remove the heart with beat
deliberate, a subject of recall.

> The poet sighs but not for what he sighs:
> His object lingers after sighing dies.

AVE ATQUE VALE

Three things there are that I must do
before I dare to die: confess
my many sins, redress
the wrongs that I have done to you
and others, and next not think
of all I might have done and didn't.
Then death. Gone in a blink
into what must seem to us a blank.
But I, like pensive Pascal,
am betting that's not all.

AGENBITE OF INWIT

Old sinners lose the hope
that they will ever change
knowing the self that others know
is only an imposter.
If I were known by others
as I am known to God
God knows if they could stand it.
Thrown stones all boomerang,
the writing in the sand will not wash away,
for mercy and not justice let us pray.

IN MEMORIAM

In the evening of the year
brittle trees give up their leaves,
over the dying grass wind grieves
crying golden coin like tears.

They settle on your grave like flowers
against the chiseled stone they lean
the world is dying as all the hours
have died since you have been.

SOLES OCCIDERE

How often suns
in dying soften
darkness; twilit
hours to the carcass
of a day lend tints
as if in recompense.

Aging I decline
like a scholar paging
Catullus in search
of an ultimate chorus
blending high and low,
and almost wish to go.

IN CEDAR GROVE

Only death could part us
and it did
for she is dead.
Time bears away the moment when
life ended and eternity began.
My grieving heart has
yet to still but beats on
systole
diastole
counting moments that no longer measure
her duration. How alien pleasure
seems when one feels pain,
the pain she has escaped at last
leaving it to me with all our past.

VI

CRITIQUE OF PURE REASON

He got up in the morning, he went to bed at night,
And sometimes the reverse,
But during all his waking hours his thought
Was on the universe.

He thought about its future, he thought about its past,
Its age he calculated as
Some zillion trillion billion million years at least,
And maybe more than that.

The cosmos in his view continued on and on and on,
Its author was Anon
And so there was no need to search for any cause
Though it has laws.

Such knowledge as we gain at school
Is minuscule,
Mankind has taken only baby steps from ignorance
And must advance.

"Though we make monkeys of our ancestors,"
He added, with gestures,
"We shall be pygmies to our progeny,
Just wait and see.

—VI

Why, in a couple thousand years or so
We shall know
Ever so much more, and I for one am glad to say
I long to see that day."

At which, he gasped and clutched his chest
And entered into more or less eternal rest.

WHY AM I SO WONDERFUL?

Life was never peachy
For Friedrich Nietzsche
Who proclaimed himself the Superman
In elegantly Gothic German.*

* This self-description is passing strange
Since he had no phone booth in which to change.

HAVING A BAWL

Don't cry for me, Pagliacci,
not that I think you will
sorrow's cry is *eccomi!*

You invite my sympathy
but if I weep as well
I grieve like you in a private hell.

RONDELET

    The clouds above
Move in the cool blue sky.
    The clouds above
Are fickle as amorphous love
    And that of course is why
They darken and begin to cry,
    The clouds above.

THE LOSER

In the game of life
he was the two of clubs
no trump was needed
to take him out.
His partner with a pout
surveyed her hand, conceded
loss, did not excuse his flubs,
was caustic as a wife.

The safest role was dummy
when the bid was made or lost
independently of him. Let others
play the prophet and predict success
his goal was ever less
for his cap he sought no feathers
but accepted just the cost
easiest on his tummy.

Best of all was solitaire
when of defeat he was alone aware.

A PROPOSITION

Letters in a line are read
from left to right
as clocks go clockwise
from day till night.

The sun from east to west
declines to set
so wouldn't it be best
that we who met

in afternoon should vespers
sing, and when
the evening whispers
join in compline?

b. v. ~b

That existential insect the bee
in the immobility of flight
fawns on flora tirelessly

fleetly fecundating he
deflowers with minimal foresight
and fawns on flora tirelessly

forming an odd ménage à three
but hiveward hies at fall of night
that exstential insect the bee

to honeyed dreams wherein
in imaginary rite
he fawns on flora tirelessly.

His is an odd immortality
fathering flowers with all his might
that existential insect the bee
fawning on flora tirelessly.

SONG

Wink at me only with thine eyes
and mine shall crosséd be
flutter your lashes if you please
and I will smile at thee.

Such mocking of your magic can
no solid solace give
nor does your presence less unman
though I feign to forgive.

Love when asymmetrical
is deep as hell and you
hang there like an icicle
my sun can never thaw.

Man they say is made for woman
and I would be your man
but you are Greek and I am Roman
and you behind your fan

lower no lids for me at all
nor ever will be mine
so since I cannot you enthral
then I shall ask for wine.

A MORAL TALE

The cardinal's catamite complained
As did the mistress of the same
That concupiscence from which their lord refrained
But seldom conduces to bitter shame.

Their charms competed for his lust
With comparable success
But artful tricks in alternation must
Tend inevitably to excess.

Ah, who more than the libertine
Knows asceticism's lure
Or who as much as the impure
Can dream of being clean?

In the end, be the phrase allowed,
These instruments of passion found
In one another teloi of a vowed
Reciprocity, naturally sound.

His Eminence, repentant, even sorry,
Ended in a Trappist monastery.

QUERY

Name a tune that's as unique
as *eine kleine nachtmusik*
or an epic, god-a-mercy,
equal to the Odyssey.

Plays and poems and paintings even
that admit no even-stephen
chip a niche in memory,
so who's your sweetie, him or me?

THE FRIENDLY SKIES

The passenger beside me settles in
the battle for the armrest can begin.
I abhor his pusillanimous intent
even as I struggle to prevent
his elbow from dislodging mine.
Meanwhile, upward through the clouds we climb.

IN THE END

The infirmity of noble minds
Is often first and this reminds
Us that the well-turned phrase
While accusing offers praise.

Diffidence may be inverted pride
And losses over which we sighed
Become possessions cherished, for
Dispatched returns the battledore.

To win and lose converge and we
Live on immersed in mystery.

AB OVO

Call no man father –
except the one who sired you
as well as God the Father who
made him and your mother.

You know, on second thought
there are many you might blame
for the fact that you exist. To name
a few . . . but why begin? You ought

to ponder your dependence on a plethora
of causes, factors, conditions, etc.
and after pondering conclude
that feigned parthenogenesis is rude.

SINS OF THOUGHT

In the aula maxima I heard
        in many twisted tongues
arguments whose inferred
        conclusions righted wrongs

yet to be committed, obiter
        dicta too wittily opined
and only by a millimeter
        false. Many have sinned

in deed if not in thought
        so weak is all mankind
but thinking is more fraught
        with danger, for the mind

when blind, unlike the eye
        that cannot see,
continues to lead us subtly
        into fallacy.

METEMPSYCHOSIS

If I were someone else and you were too
and you were me and I were you
then I (now you) would understand perhaps why I
as you am unattractive to your eye.

But if your eye were mine, its object
you, your heart would throb with love;
but I suppose that you'd object
that if we made this hypothetical move

in trading selves our souls would be involved
and we in altering so
would be effectively dissolved;
for us to lose our souls is no

small matter. Our metaphysical fling
thus finally comes to nothing –
if you indeed were me and I were you,
if you were someone else and I was too.

RESPONDEO

He said that life is a long fall from a tall
building; we plummet to our death.
But wings unfold, protest descent,
we gyre and climb, denying gravity
with song that rides like life on breath.
We do not love our dying fall
nor to our mortal fate consent
but in time mimic eternity.

Look how the falling leaves already dead
wheel in a windless air, describe
peculiar patterns as they drop, singular
descents that seek and yet postpone
coming to rest on earth where one
and all, brown, gold, red,
they will as mulch bribe
death to father forth spectacular

springs of green. So I when dust
will in my children's children fall contest.

About the Author

Author of two previous volumes, *Abecedary: An Antic Alphabet* and *Shakespearean Variations*, Ralph McInerny, like Socrates, obeys his daemon and continues to compose verse while waiting for his ship to come in. *The Soul of Wit* contains poems which are the product of age, if not wisdom, and tend to be both brief and formalist.